This book belongs

ALFR
NOBEL

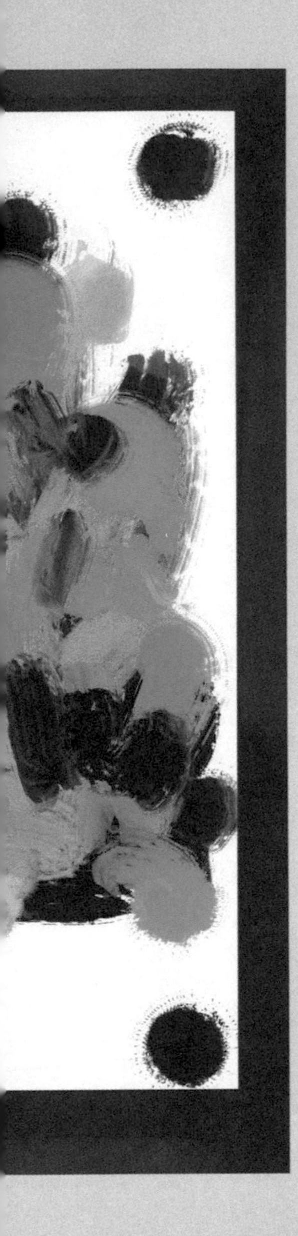

This book is dedicated to my children - Mikey, Kobe, and Jojo.

 Please send bulk order requests to growgritpress@gmail.com
978-1-63731-166-0 Printed and bound in the USA. MiniMovers.tv

Frida Kahlo

By Mary Nhin

Pictures By
Yuliia Zolotova

Hi, I'm Frida Kahlo.

I've experienced a lot of misfortune in my life, but I refused to let it keep me down.

Instead, I allowed art to ignite a passion inside of me.

When I was six years old, I became ill with polio which left me with a disability in my leg. The illness made my right leg shorter and thinner than the left! From then on, I always walked with a limp. This is part of the reason I always wore long dresses.

During this time, my father was a beacon of hope. He was a photographer and painter. He taught me about literature, nature, and philosophy.

Despite the fact that sports was seen as unsuitable for girls, he encouraged me to play sports to regain my strength. He also taught me photography. I learned how to retouch, develop, and color photographs.

I started school later than my peers because I'd been sick for so long. When I did start school, I got into trouble because I had a rebellious nature.

But then, I changed schools. It was a preparatory school that had only just started accepting girls.

It was a big school, but there were only 35 children who were girls.

Things started to turn around for me. I began enjoying learning, especially about the culture of my home nation, Mexico. I also liked matters of politics and justice.
I often admired the work of a fellow student, Diego Rivera, who was creating a mural called *The Creation* on the school campus.
I'm going to marry him someday.

I wanted to become a doctor, so I knew that I had to get good grades. Sadly, my dreams of becoming a doctor ended after a bad accident.

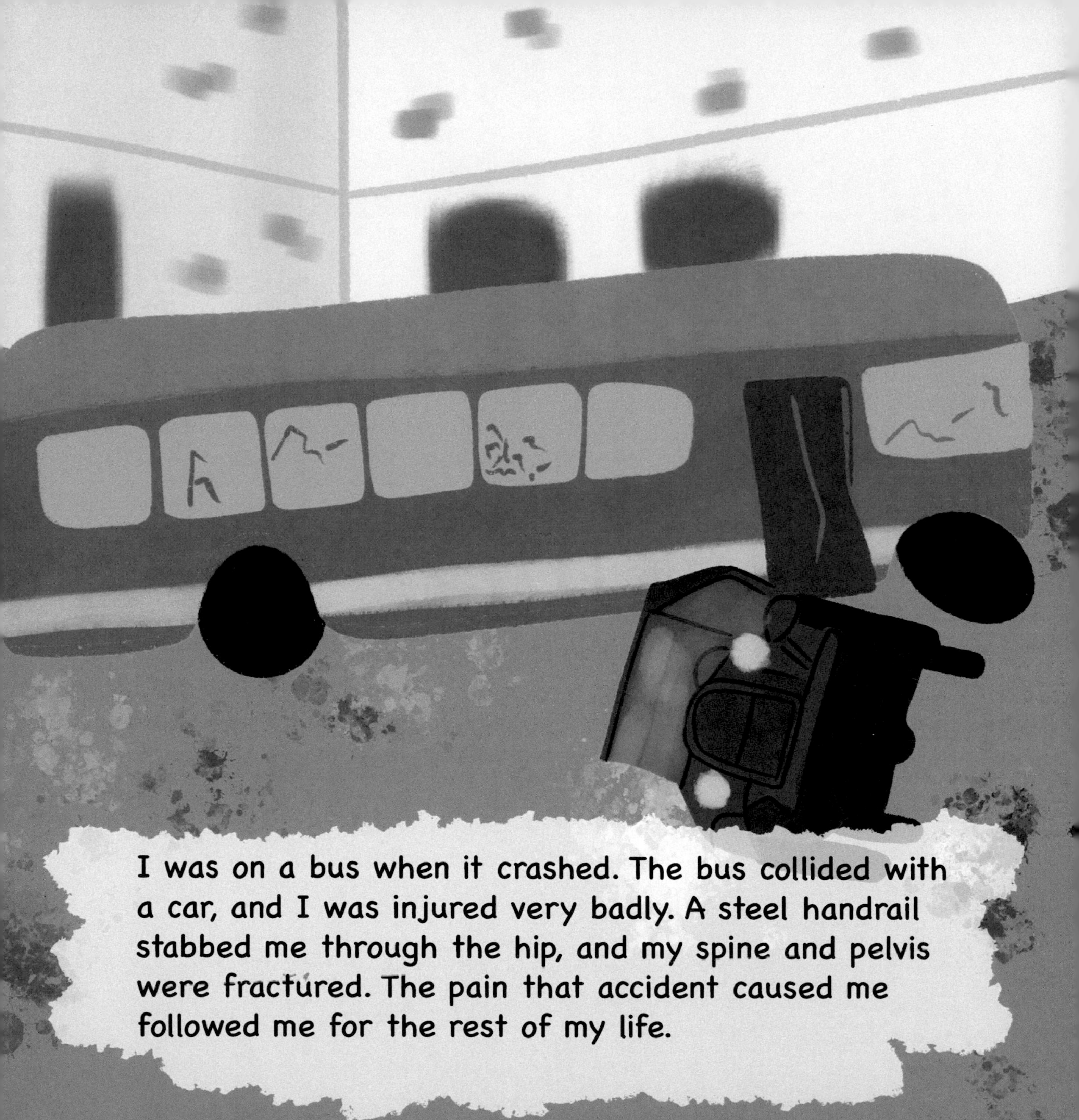
I was on a bus when it crashed. The bus collided with a car, and I was injured very badly. A steel handrail stabbed me through the hip, and my spine and pelvis were fractured. The pain that accident caused me followed me for the rest of my life.

I was confined to a bed for a very long time before I could walk again. My parents encouraged me to paint and made a special easel for me so I could do so in bed. They, also, gave me brushes and boxes of paints, and even put a mirror on the ceiling so I could see myself.

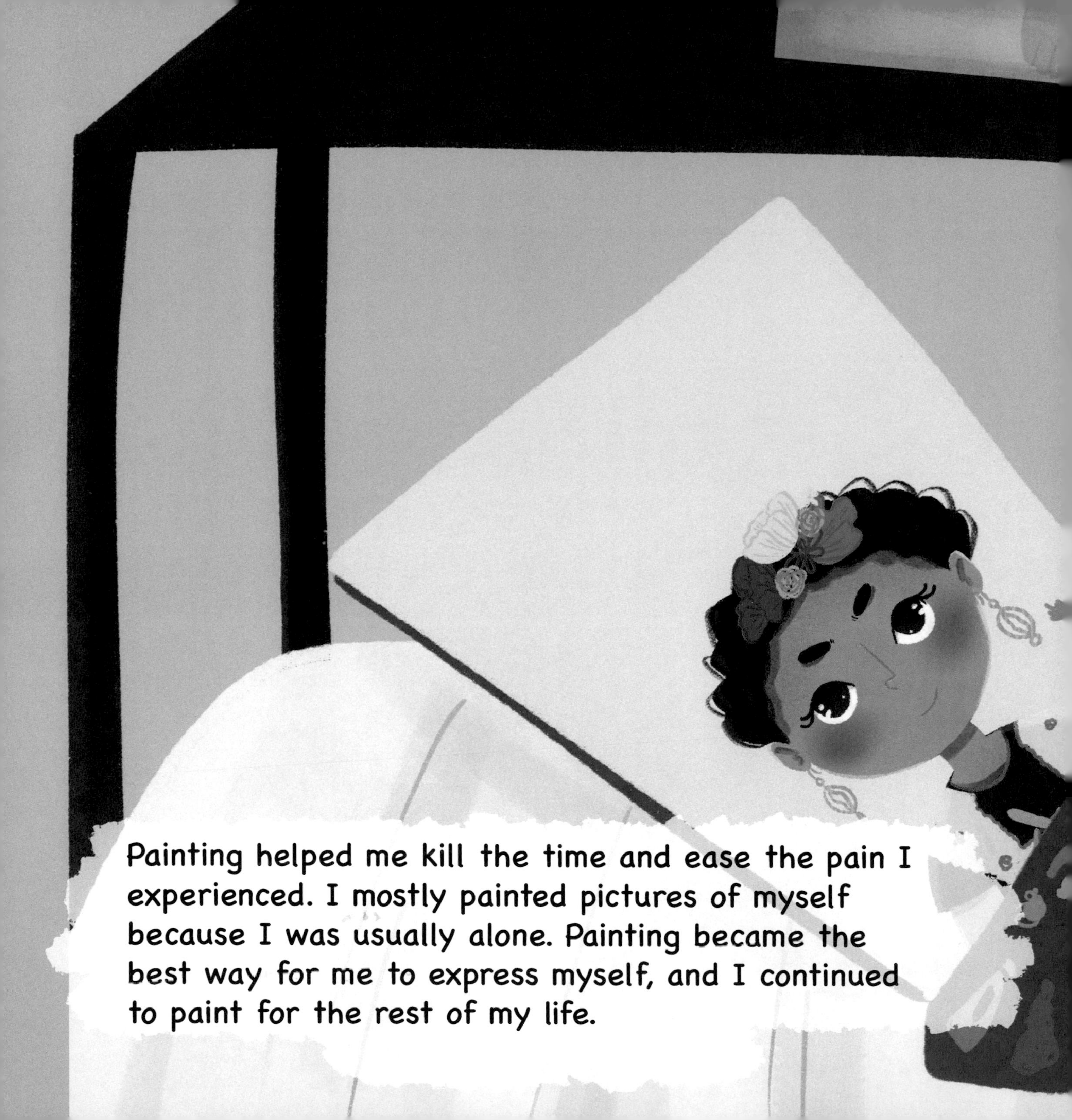

Painting helped me kill the time and ease the pain I experienced. I mostly painted pictures of myself because I was usually alone. Painting became the best way for me to express myself, and I continued to paint for the rest of my life.

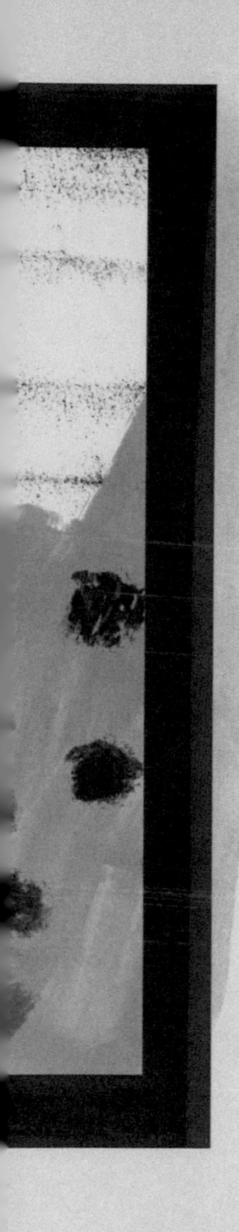

My art began to receive recognition! My first solo exhibition was at the Julien Levy Gallery in New York in 1938. It was a success!

Soon after, the Louvre Museum purchased one of my paintings, *The Frame*, making me the first Mexican artist to be featured in their collection.

I was asked to paint murals in many famous places. I traveled often for my art and to continue my efforts to campaign for social and political justice.

My paintings have broken records for Latin American art.

I became the first Latin American artist to break the one-million-dollar threshold when *Diego and I* was auctioned off for over one million dollars. In 2006, *Roots* sold for US $5.6 million, and in 2016, *Two Lovers in a Forest* sold for $8 million. Even with all the success, one of my favorite things to do was to teach younger students at an art school. This made me very happy!

Passion is the bridge that takes you from pain to change.

Timeline

1925 – Frida is injured in a bus accident

1937 – Frida's paintings are included in her first exhibit in Mexico

1938 – Frida has her first solo exhibit at the Julien Levy Gallery in New York

minimovers.tv

@marynhin @GrowGrit
#minimoversandshakers

Mary Nhin Grow Grit

Grow Grit

ALFR
NOBEL

Made in the USA
Coppell, TX
31 May 2023